# BIRMINGH

# SHOPS

## Alton & Jo Douglas

This book is ...turned on or before the last ...
... m ... it is requested

© 1992 Alton and Jo Douglas
ISBN  1  85858  002  1
Published by Brewin Books, Doric House, Church Street, Studley, Warwickshire B80 7LG.
Printed by Warwick Printing Co. Ltd., Theatre Street, Warwick CV34 4DR.
Layout by Alton and Jo Douglas
All Rights Reserved
7th Impression – January 1998

Parade, with Edward Street on the right, August 1967.

Front cover:

Exeter Road/Hubert Road, Selly Oak, December 1963.

Bull Street, with Lewis's on the left, December 1954.

IMPORTANT NOTE:

When a caption refers to something on the left or right we mean YOUR left or right as you look at the photograph.

# BREWIN BOOKS

Doric House, Church Street
Studley, Warwickshire B80 7LG

Tel: 052 785 4228  Fax: 052 785 2746

*Dear Nostalgic,*

*When Jo and I entered the book world, eleven years ago, we never imagined, in our wildest fantasies, that we'd reach number 20 - but here it is - and it's a book bursting with memories for everyone! Shops have always been focal points for the various communities and for lots of anecdotes too. I remember going into a very small corner shop, standing behind two rather large ladies and hearing one of them say, " 'ere George, you'll have to get a bigger shop". Without thinking, I muttered, "Or smaller customers" and then found myself slinking out, under their withering looks, without being served.*

*After discussing our books, at signing sessions and personal appearances, we've discovered that the major area of interest seems to be the fifties and sixties, so we've concentrated a lot of our attention on that period. However, you'll also discover some lovely historic images and a collection of interesting contemporary ones too. Enjoy yourself.*

*Yours, in friendship,*

*Alton*

The Jarvis family, outside grandma's shop, prepare to set off for a day's outing, Little King Street, Hockley, 1924

- and then, in one of the most remarkable pairs of pictures we've ever come across, in 1954, the latter-day family pose in exactly the same spot. What makes it even more fascinating is that the baby, seen in the first picture, becomes the grown-up Vera Bridges (now Woodfield) sitting second right. In front of her are her two sons, Brian and Keith. The family business ran for over half-a-century. The shop closed in 1956 and in 1959 the area was demolished and a tower block built on the site.

3

Alum Rock Road, Saltley, c. 1885.

Bournville Lane, Stirchley, 1890.

Albert Gower cycles to the shops, Coventry Road, Small Heath, 1904.

Mrs. Perkins, with her daughters Alice and Phoebe, Warwick Road, Tyseley, 1908. The shop was between Roma Road and Manor Farm Road and most of the custom came from the men working at the engine sheds.

Mrs Jane Tomkinson and her daughters Jenny and Doris, (with Patch), 15 Cattell Road, Bordesley Green, June 1911. The shop was decorated to commemorate the Coronation of King George V.

John Henry Coxell, Jnr., 27 Taunton Road, Sparkbrook, c. 1910.

High Street, Saltley, 1914.

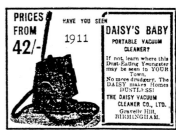

5

Nell and her mother, Mrs Flora Wright, waiting to greet customers to their tea and coffee house in Hospital Street, Hockley, 1920.

John Frost's original shop, 86 Park Road, Nechells, 1925. There are now four Frost shops in Sutton Coldfield.

Coventry Road, opposite Victoria Park, Small Heath, c. 1923.

Stratford Road, Sparkhill, c. 1926.

Ladypool Road, Balsall Heath, 1927.

Winners of the Imperial Fruit Show Window Dressing Competition, the arrangement is by Samuel and Ellen Coxell, 782 Stratford Road, Sparkhill, 1928.

Shufflebotham's grocery stores, 136/138 Alcester Road, Moseley, c. 1930.

Ellen Street, off Spring Hill, 1930.

Herbert Road/Coventry Road, Bordesley, 1930.

9

Great Francis Street/Newdegate Street, Vauxhall, 1931.

Birchfield Road, Perry Barr, 1932.

Gower's stores, 262/4 Lozells Road, just opposite the Villa Cross Cinema, Handsworth, 1934.

Stratford Road, Sparkbrook, 1933.

Mr and Mrs Herbert, along with the delivery boys and the male collectors (who went around on Sunday mornings collecting the customers' monies), Hollybank Road, Kings Heath, 1933. The shop was opposite the Tudor Cinema.

The Herberts were also the winners of the 1936 Radio Times' National Competition to see which newsagent could gain the biggest percentage rise in sales. Their assistant, Reg Davies, stands by the leaning tower of magazines.

High Street, Erdington, c. 1935.

13

High Street, Deritend, with Heath Mill Lane on the left, 1937. Possibly the city's oldest building, Ye Olde Crown, is still standing today.

## Last-Minute Rush

Birmingham folk seem to have been slow this year in getting into their stride, so to speak, for the Christmas shopping. It had been anticipated that with more money about in view of the general prosperity that has been enjoyed there would be a great rush of Christmas trade. For a time these hopes did not materialise and shopkeepers began to look glum.

But this week there has been a great change. In these last few days the streets and shops have presented scenes of extraordinary animation. The Christmas "avalanche" has come with a vengeance, said one shop assistant, who added that she had had the busiest time of her life. If they were "slow off the mark," Birmingham shoppers have certainly been making up for lost time.

## Well Wrapped Up

And talking of shopping, I wonder if it has ever been computed how many tons of wrapping paper are used in the shops of Birmingham during the Christmas period. The total figure must be phenomenal and much more to-day than was ever the case in the past. Manufacturers seem to have a perfect mania for enveloping their goods in protective coverings until to get at the article required is almost like penetrating to the heart of one of those little Chinese nests of boxes we used to see.

On top of the paper comes the ubiquitous cellophane—I beg its pardon, transparent cellulose sheeting—and finally the brown paper that the shopkeeper himself uses to complete the package. No wonder the table on Christmas morning loooks as though it had been snowing reams of paper! No wonder there is a shortage of wood-pulp!

1937

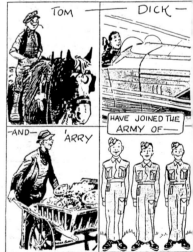
\*   \*   \*

WHEN I met Dumb Dora on Thursday we got talking about this modern steel furniture, and I said I wasn't too keen on it.
 "I can't make myself comfortable in one of those new chromium-plated chairs," I said.
 "Oh, I can."
 "How?"
 "I just put a boy friend in one before I sit down." 1940

\*   \*   \*

DAILY TELEGRAPH & MORNING POST, Monday, July 15, 1940

THE HOUSEWIVES HELP-MEAT H·P SAUCE

Queuing to buy horse meat, Dudley Road, Winson Green, during the Second World War.

Little Green Lane, Bordesley Green, 21st April 1941.

Stratford Road/Weatheroak Road, Sparkhill, 22nd November 1940.

The Home Guard on practise manoeuvres in the city, 1941. Note the boarded-up shop in the centre and the chap abseiling on the left (although he would never have known that word half-a-century ago!).

Co-op employees form their own Fire Brigade, Great Brook Street, Nechells, May 1941. The pub on the right is the "Army and Navy".

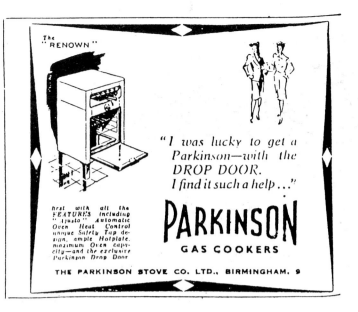

## Bread to be More Digestible

Bread is to be made more digestible by getting rid of some of the bran in the flour. Only about one-fifth of bran is digestible by human beings.

The new process will release an extra 150,000 tons of offal for feeding cattle.     1944

16.5.45

# Birmingham to issue new ration books 28 May

DISTRIBUTION of about 1,000,000 new ration books—for the next yearly period beginning on Sunday, 22 July—will start in Birmingham on Monday, 28 May.

Birmingham's Food Executive Officer (Mr. D. Lewis Grant) has arranged for the issue to be made from 13 centres which will be spread over six weeks—until 7 July, except in the case of the Civic Centre, where the new books may be obtained after that date.

Getting supplies to the shops proves difficult, Tame Road/Brookvale Road, Witton, March 1947.

17

Some of the staff of Moyle & Adams,
474 Witton Road, Witton, 1948.

Edwards Road, Erdington, 1948.

Friston Street/Ledsam Street,
Ladywood, 1949.

Birmingham Co-operative Society, Cregoe Street, Edgbaston, September 1948. This was the year that the company began turning a lot of their stores into self-service establishments.

Stocking and Shoe REPAIRS

HARRY H. PAYNE
LIMITED

Looking from Waterworks Street, with Sutherland Street on the left and ahead the continuation into Aston Hall Road, Aston, March 1949.

Walsall Road, opposite the crematorium, Perry Barr, June 1949.

19

Court Road/Edward Road, Balsall Heath,
August 1949.

Great Hampton Row/New John Street
West, Hockley, October 1949.

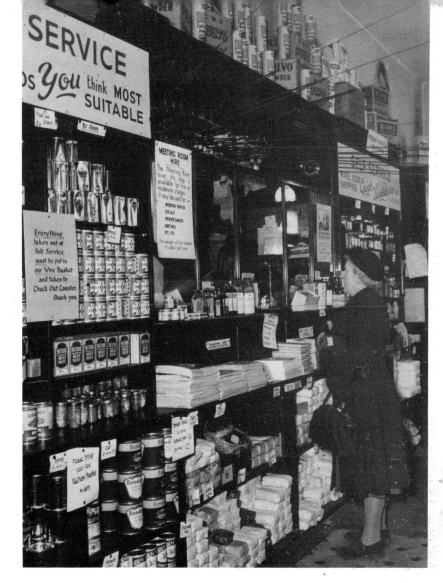

The Co-op, Stoney Lane, Yardley, April 1950. Ever since we began researching this book we have been asked, time and again, to include a picture of the "change on the wires". The assistant would place the customer's money into a small container, pull a handle and it would whizz along wires suspended above head height to the cash desk. The cashier would then send the change flying back along the pulley network. It was known as the Lamson system.

Stechford Lane, Stechford, December 1951.

Poolway, Kents Moat, August 1950.

Slade Road, Erdington, August 1950.

Coventry Road, Sheldon, c. 1950.

York Road, Kings Heath, November 1950.

Sand Pits, November 1950.

High Street, with Gate Street on the right, Saltley, January 1951.

Warwick Road, Acocks Green, September 1951. Dudley Park Road is on the left and the Post Office on the right.

Spring Hill, September 1951.

High Street, Kings Heath, December 1951. The Kingsway Cinema is on the extreme right.

Heath Street, with Winson Street just eerily visible on the left, Winson Green, December 1951.

Medley Road/Warwick Road, Greet, January 1953.

The Green, Kings Norton, December 1952.

Bloomsbury Street, with Saltley Road on the right, Hyde Park Corner, Nechells, February 1953.

Gravelly Lane, Erdington, May 1953.

Brook Hill Road, Alum Rock, June 1953.   The Co-op is decorated to herald the Coronation.

Lodge Road, Hockley, January 1954.

Islington Row, with Tennant Street on the left, Five Ways, February 1954.

Alcester Road, with Tudor Road on the left,
Moseley, February 1954.

Parade, March 1954.

Haunch Lane, Kings Heath, February 1954.

Gravelly Hill, with Leamington Road on the
left, Salford Bridge, March 1954.

High Street, Kings Heath, March 1954.

Hagley Road West, looking towards the City Centre, Quinton, May 1954.

Weoley Castle Road, Weoley Castle, July 1954.

Kitts Green Road, Kitts Green, October 1954.

Iron Lane/Stechford Road, Stechford,
September 1954.

Icknield Street/Hockley Hill,
Hockley Brook, October 1954.

St Mary's Row, Moseley,
October 1954.

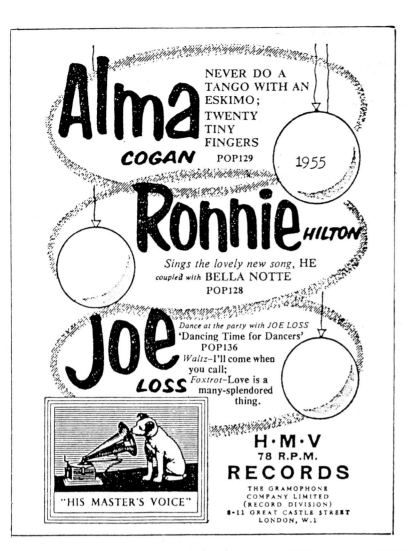

Alma Cogan.

Ronnie Hilton.

Joe Loss.

Station Road, Stechford, January 1955.

Potters Hill, Aston, January 1955.

Bristol Road South, with Rochester Road on the left, Northfield, August 1955.

29

School Road, Yardley Wood, November 1955.

Whitmore Road, with Coventry Road on the right, Small Heath, November 1955.

Garretts Green Lane, Sheldon, September 1955.

King Edward's Road/Monument Road, Ladywood, January 1956.

31

Hingeston Street/George Street West/
Prescott Street, Hockley, 1956.

Station Road, Acocks Green,
February 1956.

Aston Church Road/Chartist Road,
Saltley, January 1956.

Sheldon Heath Road, Sheldon, June 1956.

Robin Hood Lane, Hall Green, July 1956.

Great King Street, with the imposing People's Chapel Baptist Church, Hockley, December 1956.

960/2 Yardley Wood Road, Yardley Wood, January 1957.

Hagley Road, with Ladywood Road on the right, Five Ways, March 1957.

Golden Hillock Road, Small Heath, July 1957.

Wyndhurst Road, Stechford, October 1957.

Green Lane, with Bertram Road on the left, Small Heath, November 1957.

Harborne Lane, Harborne, September 1957.

Kettlehouse Road, Kingstanding, November 1957.

## Cheaper bacon in city shops
### UP TO 8d. A LB

"Bacon cheaper" said notices in many Birmingham shop windows today. Local opinion was that the downward trend in prices would be held until after Christmas, although it depended on the stocks of imported bacon which have relieved the poor supply position.

Compared with a fortnight ago, bacon prices are about 4d. per lb. cheaper and up to 8d. a lb. cheaper for some cuts.

Reports of a fall in egg prices were described by a wholesaler today as "rather misleading." He said an easing of prices had been reflected in market reports already and it was impossible to forecast the levels one day ahead. This was because egg prices were controlled by the Ministry of Food.

Bromford Lane, Bromford, January 1958.

Pip Vaughan stops outside Mrs Annie Davies's shop, Great Brook Street, Nechells, 1958.

Washwood Heath Road, Ward End, February 1958.

Weoley Avenue, Selly Oak, March 1958.

Bordesley Green/Victoria Street, Bordesley Green, May 1958.

Barnes Hill, Weoley Castle, July 1958. The Weoley Cinema, next door
to the Co-op, closed three years later.

Upper Portland Street/Lichfield Road, Aston, 1958.

Preston Road/Handsworth New Road, Winson Green, 1958.

Pershore Road, just opposite Bewdley Road, Ten Acres, 1958.

Silver Street, Kings Heath, December 1958.

Yardley Road, Acocks Green, April 1959.

Alum Rock Road, Alum Rock, 1959.

Heeley Road/Raddlebarn Road/ Umberslade Road, Selly Oak, February 1960.

Ken Dodd in a kissing mood in a Co-op store, c. 1960. Close scrutiny reveals that, even at this early stage in his career, a lot of the gags were written on the back of his hand!

Beeches Road, Great Barr, 1960.

Great Lister Street, Nechells, March 1960.

St Luke's Road/Hanover Street, Highgate, March 1960.

Bell Lane/Bristol Road South, Northfield, May 1960.

Vaughton Street, Highgate, May 1960.

Alcester Road, Moseley, June 1960.

Egghill Lane, Northfield, July 1960.

Allesley Street/Aston Road/Bracebridge Street,
Aston, September 1960.

Brewery Street/Holyhead Road, Handsworth,
November 1960.

45

Clements Road, Yardley, November 1960.

High Street, Harborne, 1960.

BYWATERS
DELICIOUS PORK
PIES & SAUSAGES

TAKE SOME HOME TODAY

OBTAINABLE
FROM OUR OWN SHOPS & AGENTS

"I LIKE TO GO OUT WITH
THE LADS AT WEEKENDS!"
I MUST buy a
NEW
BIKE

Holidays....
camping ....
it's a
wonderful
life with
a bicycle.

EASIER THAN EVER EASY TERMS
See your Dealer Now!

Join the new mobility
ON THE PHILLIPS Panda 1959

THE 49 c.c. MOPED
WITH THE HAND
OPERATED CLUTCH

The Panda is the
Aristocrat of single
Gear Mopeds. Sur-
prising power and
reliability — and the
hand operated clutch
means easy starting
and quick getaway.

51 GNS Tax Paid
Easy Terms available

A UNIT OF THE
CYCLE DIVISION

Write for Illustrated Folder to
PHILLIPS CYCLES LTD., (Dept. P4) BIRMINGHAM 40

Witton Road, with Nelson Road on
the left, Aston, December 1960.

Bristol Road South, Northfield, January 1961. This site now forms part of the Grosvenor Shopping Centre, which opened ten years later.

Rookery Road, Handsworth, February 1961.

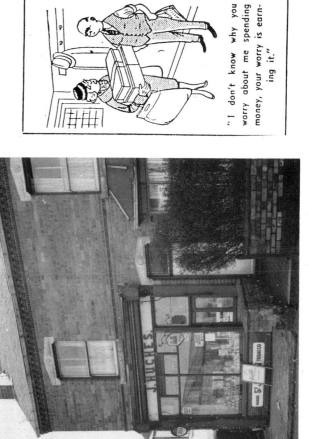

Berkeley Road East, Hay Mills, March 1961.

Farm Road, Sparkbrook, 1961.

Hurst Lane, Shard End, May 1961.

Ryland Street, Ladywood, August 1961.

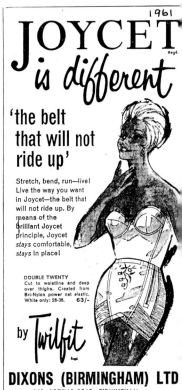
Irving Street, Lee Bank,
September 1961.

Pershore Road, Stirchley, September 1961.

...tley Road, with Cato Street North on the left, Saltley, September 1961.

FROM
CLASSIC

TO
ZODIAC

& ALL THINGS

**FORD**

ITS

**BURGESS &
GARFIELD LTD**

DISTRIBUTORS

AT COVENTRY ROAD, YARDLEY & SHELDON

Telephone: ACO 0677

Bordesley Green/ Blake Lane, opposite the site of the Era Cinema, which had closed three years earlier, April 1962.

Shirley Road, Hall Green, December 1961.

Witton Lodge Road/Wendover Road, Perry Common, January 1962.

Tarry Road/Nansen Road, Saltley, January 1962.

Tile Cross Road, Sheldon, January 1962.

Bristol Road South, Rubery, April 1962.

Sutton Road, with Harman Road on the left, Erdington, September 1962.

Lincoln Road North, Acocks Green, February 1962.

Finchley Road, Kingstanding, April 1962.

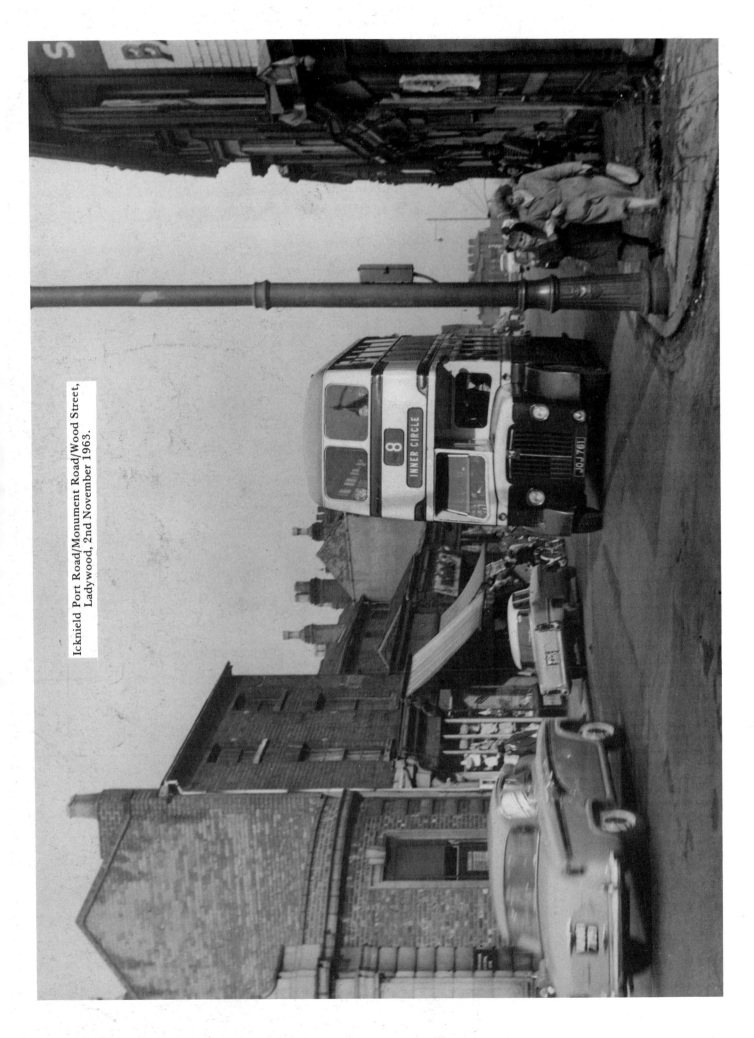

Icknield Port Road/Monument Road/Wood Street, Ladywood, 2nd November 1963.

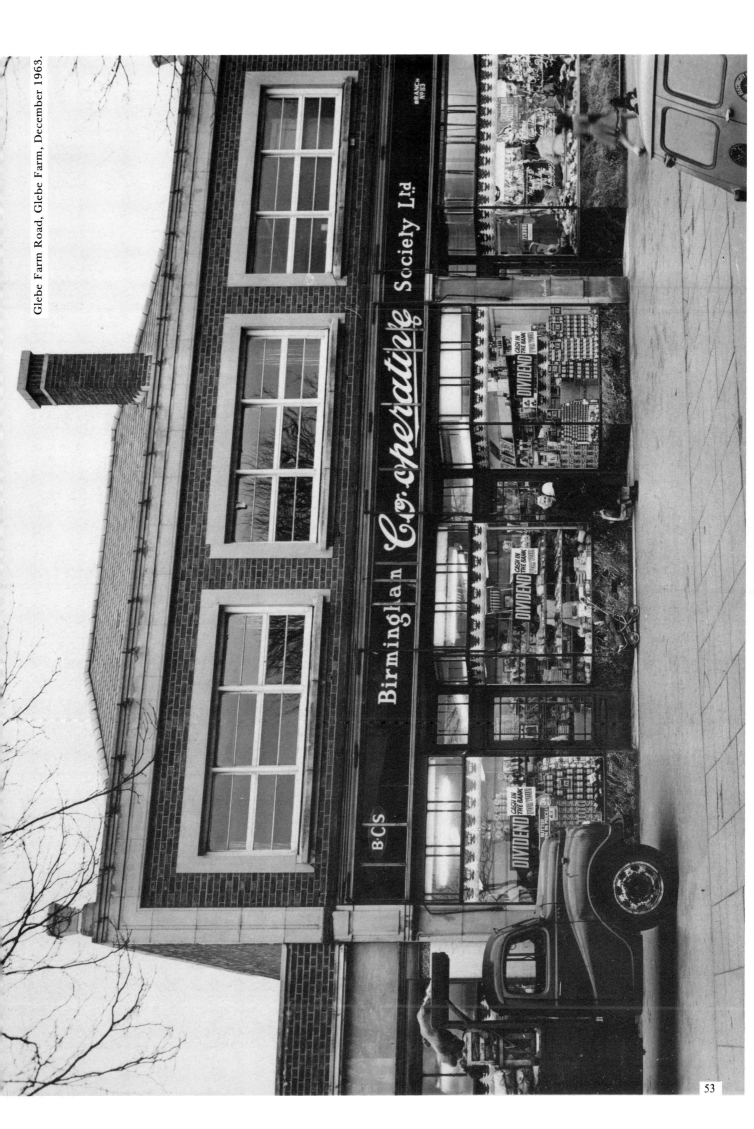

Glebe Farm Road, Glebe Farm, December 1963.

A mobile grocery van in Taylor Street, Nechells Green, 1964. Alton's mum was always amused at the sight of the customers clambering in and doing their shopping, actually inside a vehicle, parked outside her house in Small Heath!

Crompton Road, Handsworth, 1963.

Jiggins Lane, Bartley Green, March 1963.

# Shoppers start stamp collecting

1963

THE introduction of trading stamps brought a new kind of cut-price war in the supermarkets.

It also produced a novel way of buying Christmas presents. For free, if you were lucky enough to be a long distance lorry driver.

## Bedspread

One such driver called at a Birmingham shop with an empty suitcase and a pocketful of 20 books containing 25,600 stamps.

He exchanged them for a candlewick bedspread (four books) an electric fire (10½), a child's scooter (two), a doll's crib (2½) and a tea set (one).

It had taken him 10 months to fill the books — and it didn't cost him a penny.

He collected the stamps representing the purchase of petrol totalling £630 on behalf of his employers.

Quinton Road West, Quinton, 1964.

Sladepool Farm Road, Highters Heath, June 1964.

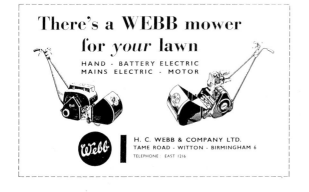

Gilbertstone Road/Coventry Road, Yardley, September 1964.

Booth's Farm Road/Perry Wood Road,
Great Barr, September 1964.

Hawthorn Road/Warren Road, Perry Barr, 1964. Little did the filmgoers at the Mayfair that week realise that "Taza, Son of Cochise", starring Rock Hudson, would be shown on television in May 1992.

Highfield Road, Hall Green, June 1964.

Speedwell Road/Kings Road, Hay Mills, September 1964.

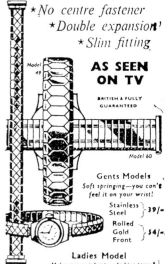

Bristol Road, with the MEB sub-station on the right, Selly Oak, 1964.

BMT Services Ltd., Kingstanding Road, Perry Barr, August 1965.

Taunton Road, Sparkbrook, February 1965.

Station Road, with Johnson Road on the left, Erdington, January 1965.

Duddeston Mill Road, Duddeston, May 1965.

Chipperfield Road/Ermington Crescent, Castle Bromwich, September 1965.

Elmbridge Road, Perry
Barr, October 1965.

Benacre Street/Gooch Street, Highgate, October 1965.

Stratford Road/Kyotts Lake Road, Sparkbrook, December 1965.

Coleshill Road, Washwood Heath, December 1965. The Beaufort Cinema was sited on the right.

Pershore Road, Kings Norton, February 1966. Incidentally, Roy Edwards was the singer who first came to fame with the Squadronaires and the Geraldo Orchestra. He later starred in ATV's "Lunch Box" with Noelle Gordon and the Jerry Allen Quartet.

Bridge Street West/Great Russell Street, Hockley, 1966.

Coventry Road/Flora
Road, Hay Mills,
September 1966.

Alvechurch Road,
West Heath, July 1967.

Victoria Road/Park
Road, Aston, June
1967.

Gerrard Street/
Berners Street, Lozells,
July 1967.

The Green, Kings Norton, October 1967. A quarter of a century later it is reassuring to find that the Pet Stores is still totally recognisable!

The Green, Kings Norton, October 1967.

Guildford Street/Gower Street, Lozells,
March 1968.

Coldbath Road, Kings Heath, May 1968. The
Daily Mirror were doing a feature on Birming-
ham, this particular week, in their series, "The
Boom Cities".

Coventry Road, with Grange Road on the left,
Small Heath, 1968.

Warren Farm Road, Kingstanding, August 1968.

Belgrave Road/Longmoor Street, Balsall Heath,
October 1968.

Moseley Road, with Belgrave Road on the right, Moseley, 1968.

The Queen and the Duke of Edinburgh arrive to unveil a plaque, at the Clock Tower, to commemorate the opening of Chelmsley Wood Shopping Centre, 7th April 1970.

# Parking on trust

12.3.70

## BUT CITY FEES MAY
## BE INCREASED

TRUST-THE-MOTOR-IST car parking is to be reintroduced in Birmingham.

But charges for using 15 municipal car parks in the city may be increased.

Birmingham Public Works Committee was today considering details of a trust-the-motorist scheme planned to be launched on a park at Alcester Road, Moseley.

Mr. Neville Borg, the city engineer and surveyor, said that it had been tried previously at the Baskerville House car park, but it was found to be an unsuitable site.

### Automatic

Drivers will be asked to obtain their own tickets from an automatic machine before driving into the car park, and there will be irregular checks by an attendant to see that tickets are displayed on windscreens.

Councillor Harold Edwards, Chairman of the Public Works Committee, said that the scheme would be introduced as an experiment on the car park at Alcester Road, which was to be re-surfaced.

If successful, it would be

Evening Mail Reporter

extended to other parks in the city.

He said: "This type of scheme would help us in providing cheaper car parking in the city. The motorists will be put on trust to pay."

### The charges

Details were being considered today by the General Purposes Committee.

It is proposed that the charge should be 6d. for a morning's parking and 6d. for an afternoon.

Coun. Edwards said that the park at Moseley was at present in bad condition.

It was intended to improve it greatly by resurfacing. The suggested charge would be cheaper than using parking meters.

A proposal that the charge

for long-stay car parks in the city should be stepped up was being put to the committee.

There are at present 15 of the parks and it costs motorists 2s. 6d. a day to leave their vehicles.

Coun. Edwards said it was being suggested that charges should be increased to 3s.

The shoppers' car park in the city centre would not be affected and would remain at 1s. an hour.

### Five years

The last time that long-stay charges were raised was 1965.

Coun. Edwards said: "We have managed to contain charges for a long time, but, unfortunately, we are faced with rising costs, including the wages of parking attendants.

"If the increases are approved we shall still be the cheapest of the big cities for parking."

Bromford Drive, Bromford Bridge, November 1970.

when you drink

*Ansells*

**The Better Beer**

you're
in good company

Bernard Youens (Stan Ogden in "Coronation Street") greets Mrs. Rosaline Whatling at the opening of Woolworth's new store, Chelmsley Wood, 26th February 1971.

### And another

ANOTHER old Birmingham name in the wine trade that vanishes from shop fronts after today is that of Innes Smith, which was founded in 1868.

Under an amalgamation some years ago, the only shop that continued to display the name was in Digbeth.

It closes tonight. From tomorrow its business will be transacted by Grants of St. James, of Lichfield Road, Aston. *1970*

Hagley Road, Edgbaston, August 1971.

# No price rise for fish and chips

**Evening Mail Reporter**

FISH and chip shop owners in the Birmingham district have decided against proposed price rises.

A mass meeting voted to keep selling chips at 9d. and 10d. as long as possible.

Mrs. Doreen Shand, secretary of the Birmingham branch of the Federation said today that friers rejected a plan to sell chips at a shilling a bag.

"They did not want to inflict price rises on their children and pensioner customers."

Instead, they are sending a telegram to Mr. Cledwyn Hughes, Minister of Agriculture, demanding action to prevent "perennial" potato shortages.

They call for an immediate review of the potato quota system.

The friers are also asking M.P.s to take up their case.

Mrs. Shand added: "Every spring fish and chip shops suffer because of a potato famine.

This year our troubles have come early because of the bad weather conditions. We want the Ministry to ensure that each year there is a potato surplus."

The fish friers will meet again on May 1 to review progress of their protests.

Shawsdale Road, Castle Bromwich, May 1972.

Walsall Road/Queslett Road, Great Barr, September 1971.

Soho Road, Handsworth, August 1971.

Muntz Street, Small Heath,
March 1974.

College Road, Erdington,
January 1973.

Kings Road, Kingstanding, January 1973.

Sycamore Road, Bournville, 26th February 1974.

Milestone Lane/Holyhead Road, Handsworth, December 1973.

Stratford Road, Hall Green, October 1974.

Oaktree Lane, Selly Oak, January 1976.

73

Vanessa Wong and Ming Leung shop at the Wing Yip Chinese Supermarket, Digbeth, 26th September 1977.

Miss Susannah Greves, at the age of 80 still running the shop her parents opened in 1912, Albert Road, Kings Heath, November 1976.

Shirt Dept., John Barrie's shop, Lower Parade, Sutton Coldfield, July 1976.

Jean Adderley and Joan Riley, normally behind the coffee bar counter at Davey's furniture store, help traders to celebrate 100 years of shopping on The Parade, Sutton Coldfield, April 1979.

Smaller shopkeepers are disappearing, with a third of Birmingham's shops having vanished in 30 years, says a report to city planners.

But old-style local High Street centres will still be the firm favourite for shoppers for the next ten years, it adds.

The report on shopping trends was prepared by city officials to help the planners to work out a policy on how shopping arrangements in the city should develop.

The report, which went before a recent planning committee meeting, said there were nearly 20,000 retail outlets, including corner shops, in Birmingham in 1950. Now there were only 12,500.

But the officials said that this did not mean there were less shopping facilities, because new traders who had opened up since, tended to have bigger premises.

The report added that planners had been under pressure to allow more big bulk-buying supermarkets on the edge of the city for car-borne shoppers, in recent years.

But it added that High Street type centres would continue being the favourite of most shoppers for the rest of the decade because of travel costs.

The committee agreed to think about giving more support to projects to revitalise declining older shopping centres in future 1980.

Jewellery Quarter, Warstone Lane, Hockley, 12th February, 1987.

Radio WM presenter, Ed Doolan, waves cheerily from the jacuzzi before presenting it to the Children's Hospital, 16th April 1987. The bath was a gift from Bill and John Landon (seated) on behalf of the Bathroom Village, Icknield Port Road, Ladywood. The company began trading on the site of the Crown Cinema in 1969. The cinema, itself, closed in 1961.

Gillian Waterson collected food worth £95 in a two minute dash around Sainsburys. It was her prize for winning a raffle, organised by Moseley Lions, to raise funds to buy a "Lifeline" alarm system for an elderly person in the city. Kings Heath, 1985.

Comedian, Don Maclean, takes the bit between his teeth to open the Children's Hospice Shop, Pershore Road, Stirchley, 15th June 1989. It was the second shop to open in support of the Acorns, in Selly Oak. Don is currently hosting a regular programme on Radio Two every Sunday morning.

One Stop Shopping Centre, Perry Barr, 1990.

Judy Osborne makes an early start, Alvechurch Road, West Heath, June 1992.

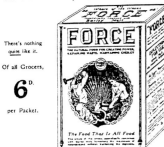

Greys, Bull Street, c. 1900

Corporation Street, from the Old Square, with Central Hall visible in the centre, Summer 1903.

Lewis's, Bull Street, 1914.

George Hastings waits for his first customer of the day, Hornes, St. Martin's Lane, 1919.

**An Egg Famine Coming.** 1917

Already " new laid eggs "—some of them, I
fear, of doubtful " newness "—are about a shilling a dozen dearer than they were at this time
last year. And next winter, I hear, there may
be an egg famine.

**And the Cause.**

The cause of the shortage, an expert tells me,
was the panic created by alarmist food declara-
tions. Breeders stopped hatching, and many
poultry-keepers disposed of their birds. I am
sorry to say that soldiers in hospital will suffer.

## THE MERE MALE OPINION IN JANUARY SALES.

It is said that, when a husband and wife go together to the sales, his advice is never by any chance taken by her. Why, then, must she take him? Would it not do equally well if she were provided with a lay figure on wheels with a string attached?

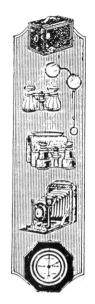

Co-op stores, from all over the city, parade along Paradise Street, 1921.

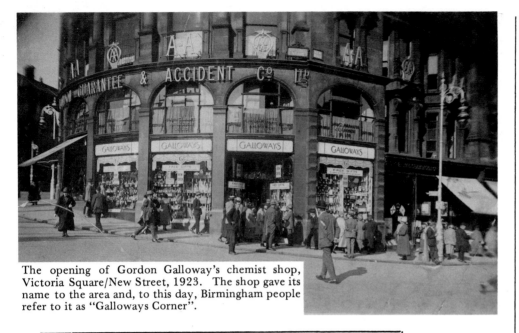

The opening of Gordon Galloway's chemist shop, Victoria Square/New Street, 1923. The shop gave its name to the area and, to this day, Birmingham people refer to it as "Galloways Corner".

Marks & Spencer open, after re-building, 42/43 High Street, 21st October 1927.

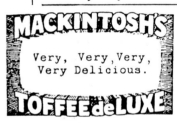
## IF PIGS COULD FLY

The sportily-clad man entered the poultry shop.

"Have you a very good pheasant? I'd like to give my wife a surprise."

"I'm afraid, sir, that I've sold out of pheasants. But how about one of these very special pork pies—your wife is sure to like it."

"Pork pie be blowed! How can I tell my wife I shot a pork pie?"

# PRIESTLEYS
## COLMORE ROW, BIRMINGHAM.

1928

**"HIS MASTER'S VOICE."**

The staff of Priestleys enjoy an evening out, 1928.

Victoria Square, c. 1928.

Bull Street, towards Colmore Row, c. 1929. The original Rackhams' store is on the left, on the corner of Temple Row.

Co-op, High Street, July 1929.

The message on the back of this postcard reads, "Could you please give fowl mash before you go back? Warm up dinner a bit"!

Corporation Street, c. 1931.

The staff of Alfred Allen, congregate in St Jude's Passage, c. 1935. The company is now situated in Bristol Street.

# WOODHOUSE'S
## GREAT JANUARY SALE
### Your Bargain Month!

RAIL AND BUS FARE PAID on COMPLETED ORDERS OF £10 OR OVER

OLD FURNITURE TAKEN in PART PAYMENT FOR NEW
BEST PRICES GIVEN

### GREAT CARPET BARGAINS

ANY CARPET FROM OUR LARGE HIGH-GRADE STOCK OF MODERN DESIGNS AND BEAUTIFUL COLOURINGS Delivered Free for—

**10%**

Heavy Seamless Axminster Carpets.

### LUXURIOUS THREE-PIECE SUITE

**5/- MONTHLY NO DEPOSIT**

Comprising 4ft. 6in. Settee and 2 Large Easy Chairs well sprung, stuffed Black Fibre, topped Hair, and covered in excellent quality Tapestry. Usual Price 17 Gns.

SALE PRICE £9-5-0
Deferred Payments Price, £9/18/6.

1936

### OUR GREAT JANUARY SALE

Is your unique Furnishing opportunity, because leading Manufacturers have co-operated with us in our attempt to offer a wider selection and better values than ever before.

You can furnish or re-furnish your home complete, with Carpets and Lino also, at prices so low and No-Deposit Terms so convenient as to be beyond expectations.

Come early and see our wonderful bargains. They will convince you that we remain supreme for the complete furnishing of modern homes at the lowest prices and easiest No-Deposit Terms.

### Full-size WALNUT BEDSTEAD COMPLETE

**5/- MONTHLY NO DEPOSIT**

With Coil Spring Mattress Overlay, Feather Bolster and Pillows. Usual Price, 9 Gns.

SALE PRICE £4-19-6
Deferred Payments Price, £5/7/6.

### EASIEST CREDIT TERMS
## NO-DEPOSIT

CASH & CREDIT PRICES Marked in PLAIN FIGURES

### HIGH-GRADE OAK BEDROOM SUITE

Comprising 3ft. Wardrobe, 2ft. 6in. Dressing Table with triple frameless mirrors, 2ft. 6in. Chest; finished a rich Antique or Tan shade. Usual price 11 Gns.

SALE PRICE 7½ Gns.
Deferred Payments Price, £8/10/0.

**5/- MONTHLY NO DEPOSIT**

Full-size Oak Bedstead to match. Sale Price, 39/6. Deferred Payments Price 42/6.

CUT OUT THIS COUPON FOR FREE BARGAIN BOOK and post in unsealed envelope with ½d stamp

NAME _____
ADDRESS _____

Free Fire and Life Insurance.

BUSINESS HOURS:
9 a.m. to 7 p.m.
Saturdays to 8 p.m.
Close Wednesdays 1 p.m.

OPEN ALL DAY SATURDAY.

## WOODHOUSE & SON
(The British and Colonial Furniture Co., Ltd.)
### 88-91, NEW STREET, BIRMINGHAM.

And at London, Manchester, Liverpool, Leeds, Huddersfield, Bradford, Sunderland, Newcastle-on-Tyne, Middlesbrough, Edinburgh, Glasgow, Southampton, Montreal, Etc.

B M 8/1/36.

## NO CONNECTION with ANY OTHER FURNISHING HOUSE in BIRMINGHAM

Bull Street, 1938, decorated to mark the centenary of the granting of the Municipal Charter to the City, (by which Birmingham legally became "a town").

New Street, 1937. Just across from the Odeon (originally the Paramount) which opened the following year, much of this area was destroyed by the fire which followed the air-raid on the 9/10th April 1941. A large marquee was erected on the site and used, for a while, for fund-raising and entertainment. The area became known to Brummies as the Big Top.

Colmore Row, showing the Great Western Arcade on the left, 23rd November 1940.

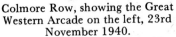

The bombed-out shell of Marks & Spencer, High Street, 11th April 1941. Seen from Union Street, the store had suffered in the air-raid three days earlier. It re-opened again in 1946.

88

## Which kind of Reader are you?

From the librarian's point of view, readers may be divided into two kinds: those who want something to read, and those who want to keep abreast of current literature.

A great many people say, in effect, "What I want is a good book. Never mind how old it is, so long as it is worth reading." Many such readers *prefer* books that have been out a few months, arguing, truly enough, that time does some useful sorting out.

But for many others, to be among the new books is essential if they are to get the most out of their reading. To them books are news, with which they must be up to date.

Which kind of reader are you? Must you have the new books, or doesn't it matter? Either way it's not expensive, but there is no point in paying more than is necessary, and W. H. Smith & Son like to feel that subscribers to their Library know exactly what they are paying for; and are getting what they want, as far as possible in a book-rationed world.

1943

## The price of books

I CHALLENGE any publisher to tell us how there is any justification for the present price of books. Why must I pay 10s. 6d. and 12s. 6d. to-day for books that I can scarcely read because they're so badly printed? These books before the war could be bought for 5s. and 7s. 6d.

I refuse to believe that the increase in the cost of paper accounts for all this, and in any case I imagine that for a variety of reasons and with staffs heavily depleted due to the call-up, publishers' and printers' overheads *per book* represent much less than they did in peace-time.

The Big Top site, photographed from High Street to New Street, December 1944. A circus and fairground is setting up, ready to catch the Christmas trade, on the bombed site.

New Street, October 1948.

Colmore Row,
February 1949.

Snow Hill, with Clive
Passage on the right,
February 1950.

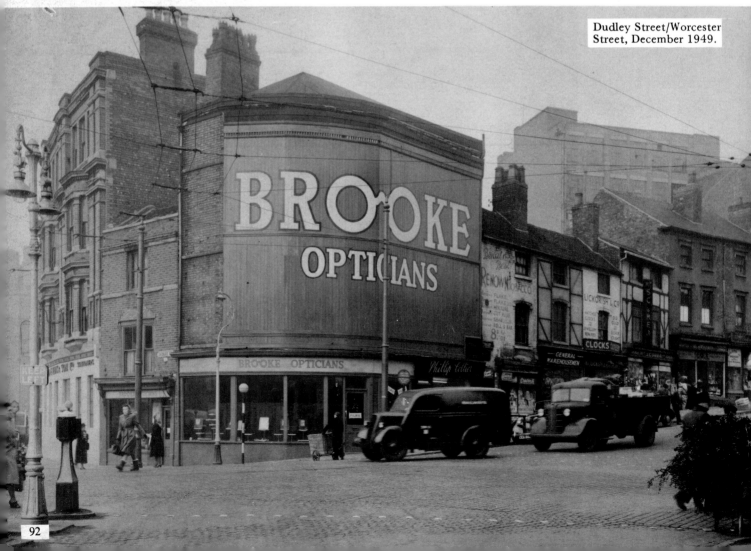

Dudley Street/Worcester
Street, December 1949.

BARROW'S STORES LIMITED

CORPORATION STREET AND BULL STREET, BIRMINGHAM, 2

TELEPHONE: CENTRAL 8686 (8 lines)    ◆    TELEGRAMS: BARROW, BIRMINGHAM, 2

WHOLESALE WAREHOUSE: LOWER PRIORY

23rd March 1949.

The Chief Reporter,
Evening Dispatch,
Corporation Street,
Birmingham, 2.

Dear Sir,

    I enclose for your information a copy
of a booklet that is being issued on Monday
next week in connection with the celebration
of the 125th anniversary of the founding of
the firm.

    I also enclose a notification of the
visit the Lord Mayor and Lady Mayoress are
paying us on Monday, 28th March, at 3.15 p.m.
to inspect the temporary reconstruction on
a small scale of R.C.Barrow's Tea, Coffee
and Spice Warehouse in Bull Street as it was
about a hundred years ago.

    Yours faithfully,

    p.p.BARROW'S STORES LIMITED,

    *R M Barrow*

    DIRECTOR.

RMB/JWB.

"Mr. Fabian, I think it's
disgraceful. I can't get a
turkey for Christmas. What
do you suggest?"
"Nuts, madam, nuts!"

Albert Street/New
Meeting Street,
November 1949.

Bull Ring, July 1952.

New Street, 30th April 1951. Just past the Arden Hotel the canopy of the Odeon Cinema can be seen jutting out, the films showing were Ann Blyth in "Our Very Own" and Victor Mature in "Gambling House".

Martineau Street, showing Union Passage, April 1952.

Ventriloquist Peter Brough, with his dummy Archie Andrews (stars of the radio series "Educating Archie") entertain the audience at the Co-op, High Street, 1952. This was part of a national safety campaign that the duo were involved in.

Spiceal Street, which ran from the Bull Ring down to the right of
St Martin's Church, January 1953.

Corporation Street/Bull Street, 13th December 1953.

Steelhouse Lane, going down towards the General Hospital, February 1954.

Possibly the largest advertising site in the city was on the corner of Suffolk Street and Navigation Street, February 1954.

Corporation Street/Lower Priory, March 1954.

Union Street, with Kunzle's Restaurant in the centre, October 1953.

Bull Street, with Dr Johnson's Passage on the right, March 1954.

Hurst Street, with Ladywell Walk on the left, October 1954.
Just across the road is the Hippodrome.

Broad Street, March 1955.

International entertainer, Max Bygraves, examines a firework display model aided by his longtime friend, Aston Villa footballer and shop owner, Harry Parkes, Worcester Street, October 1954.   Harry had a second shop at Six Ways, Erdington.   Nowadays he operates from 159 Corporation Street.

Singer, Frankie Vaughan, signs copies of his photographs and records, Dale Forty, New Street, 25th October 1955.

Mrs. Styles and Mrs. Harris in the pen department, Stanford & Mann Ltd., 72/73 New Street, after refitting had taken place, 1955. When Galloways Corner was demolished the firm moved to 34 Paradise Circus and then, in 1990, they returned to 53 New Street.

Colmore Row, 1955.

Broad Street, with Oozells Street on the left, April 1956.

Holloway Head, April 1956.

Dale End, May 1956. The Book Room is now in Carrs Lane.

New Street/Stephenson Place, 1956.

Jamaica Row/Edgbaston Street, December 1957.

Steelhouse Lane, from Snow Hill Corner, January 1957.

The Market Hall, from outside Moor Street Station, 1958.

ull Ring, 1958.

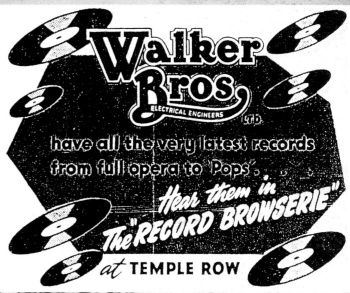

Cannon Street, September 1958.

Martineau Street/Bull Street/Dale End, seen from High Street, January 1959.

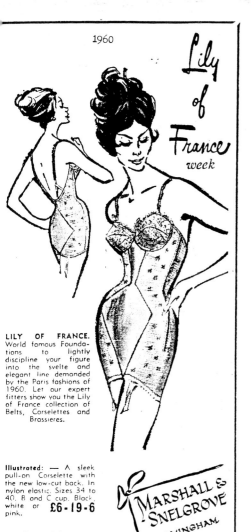

The interior of the new Boots, Big Top, where self-selection has been introduced. October 1959.

Corporation Street, showing Rackhams under construction, September 1959.

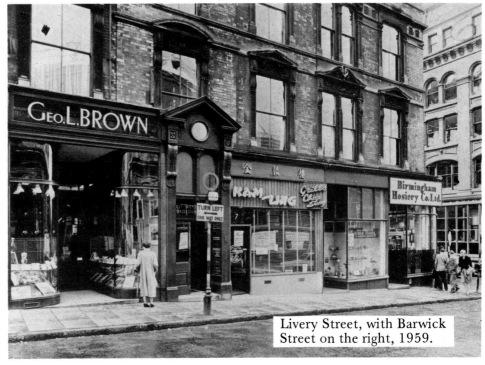

Livery Street, with Barwick Street on the right, 1959.

105

Stephenson Street, with Lower Temple Street on the left, 1960

New Street, with Lower Temple Street on the right, January 1960.

Ryder Street/Stafford Street, May 1960.

Holloway Head/Suffolk Street, March 1960.

Stafford Street, with Ryder Street going from left to right and the Central Fire Station in the distance, Dale End, October 1960.

Horse Fair, July 1961.

John Bright Street/Navigation Street, from Hill Street, January 1961.

Suffolk Street, facing Paradise Street, with Swallow Street on the right, March 1962.

A busy time at the Toy Fair, Lewis's, December 1964.

The Staff Council, Lewis's, 1963. Each year, one member of every department would be elected to the Staff Council and, during the January and July sales, they would organise the running of the entire store for one day. It was always treated as a Special Bargain Day.

A break from the shoppers as the staff relax in their lounge, Littlewoods, New Street, 19th September 1962. In the top right hand corner the girls are choosing suitable music to add to the atmosphere.

Bull Ring shoppers, 1964.

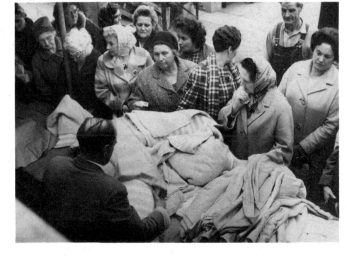

Looking south-west, from the Rotunda, 1964.

Bull Ring Shopping Centre, 1964.

The Rotunda, viewed from St Martin's Church, 1964.

One of the many routes home for shoppers, through Digbeth, 1965.

The unveiling of a street guide to the City Centre by the Lord Mayor, Alderman George Corbyn-Barrow, Stephenson Place/New Street, January 1966.

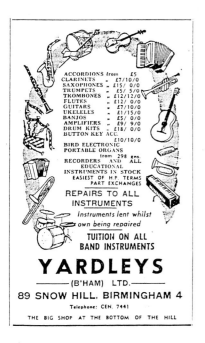

Bruce Forsyth, toasts the girls of the Birmingham Co-op, High Street, c. 1968.

Bull Street, February 1972.

# PEDESTRIANISATION

**Evening Mail Reporter**

BIRMINGHAM Chamber of Trade is urging that part of the city centre should be closed to vehicles.

The Chamber's council, on which major stores in Birmingham are represented, is asking the City Council to give immediate considera-tion to a "pedestrianisation" scheme.

Councillor R. J. Tyler, chairman of the chamber, said today: "We have come to the conclusion that pedestrianisation would solve many of the problems of the city centre.

"We feel that it is now the responsibility of the City Council, in the interests of the ratepayers, to carry out an in-depth study of all the factors involved."

The Chamber's council is writing to the Corporation urging that a working party investigate the proposal.

It suggests that there should be full consultation with all interested parties, and the views of traders and commercial firms should be obtained.

## Bus routes

It is calling for a "comprehensive survey," which would also cover such things as bus routes, traffic flow, parking sites and pedestrian access.

Mr. Tyler said: "It would be wrong to merely consider pedestrianisation in isolation. There are many associated factors which have got to be investigated if a scheme is to work successfully."

He said it might be necessary to alter bus stops and routes, for example, so that the amount of traffic using the city centre was reduced.

Mr. Tyler said the council thought a proposal recently put forward by Birmingham Junior Chamber of Commerce closing part of New Street vehicles, had "great merit."

"The traders are virtually animous in their support for idea. What is now needed thorough survey to decide best it could be done and parts of the city centre w be the most suitable.

---

## Centenary for the Beehive

MAY 1970

THE Beehive store in Priory Ringway is celebrating its centenary during Spring Festival fortnight.

It is 100 years since the Beehive began trading in the city centre and they are celebrating with a big festival splash.

The interior and windows have been bedecked with "festival fortnight" posters and colours, and the store has designed its own motif, a honeycomb, to go with the celebration slogan "100 years of family trading."

The festival will be the launching pad for a "new look" store.

The management announced the biggest re-organisation since the Beehive, the only large family-run store left in the city centre, moved into its Priory Ringway premises two years ago.

They are dropping their women's and men's fashion departments to make way for expansions to the household departments.

A statement said: "We are looking forward and planning for the 1970s and the changes in shopping habits which are bound to come."

It said that during the past 100 years of family trading, the store had been a leading name throughout the city in household goods. They had decided to concentrate on these departments and expand to give a bigger and better range for customers.

"Unfortunately, to do this, it will mean that our ladies' fashion department and also men's wear department will no longer exist.

"Our aim will be, as always, to give bigger and better selection and value for money in the years ahead."

The managing director, Mr. Ronald Knight, said that special offers were being made to housewives during the festival. These included a free curtain making-up service.

Mr. Knight said: "We are supporting the Spring Festival. It is a marvellous event which has generated great interest both among retailers and customers."

---

## Why this is going to be Birmingham's favourite yogurt

Suddenly yogurt is fun food – not just something for weight-watchers and the diet-minded. People are eating it, more and more people, just because they love it.

And the yogurt that's really taking off – the most magic, flying yogurt of them all – is Dairy Crest. Last year, we had to make half as much again as we did in 1971. This year we shall have to make even more. And why this rush to Dairy Crest? Silly question.

It tastes so good that expert judges gave it the only gold medal for real fruit yogurt at the last international Dairy Show.

But the really expert judge is you. Try two or three varieties to get you started on what should be the beginning of a beautiful relationship.

**Dairy Crest Real Fruit Yogurts** Strawberry, Raspberry, Blackcurrant, Cherry, Mandarin, Pineapple, Banana, Lemon, Apricot, Hazelnut, Raisin and Brazil Nut, and Natural.

### Dairy Crest Products.

Milk Marketing Board, Thames Ditton, Surrey

---

Proposals for closing some city centre streets to traffic are now being explored and consultants are investigating a possible system of multi-purpose traffic tunnels beneath the central area of the city.

But the city, at the moment, is still wedded to the principle of allowing the private car entry to the city centre.

More and more multi-storey car parks are planned to give a total of 25,000 parking spaces in and around the city centre. These will be accompanied next year by a big extension of the parking meter-zone.

The development of the shopping precinct has been a feature of post-war Birmingham.

The small shops lining main roads in the suburbs are being replaced by chain stores and supermarkets in traffic-free shopping centres, with their own car parks like those at Aston, Five Ways and Perry Barr. 1970

---

Temple Row, January 1974.

High Street, March 1972.

Carrs Lane, 1974.

Cherry Street, 1974.

A rainy January day in Corporation Street, 1974.

Union Street, 29th December 1976.

Christmas shoppers throng along the ramp, to and from The Birmingham Shopping Centre (now the Pallasades), December 1976.

Cliff Richard signs copies of his new book
. . . . . .

. . . . . and Enoch Powell, M.P. . . . . .

. . . . . . and comedy team, the Goodies,
Midland Educational, 1977.

Actor, Dirk Bogarde, finding new fame as an author, signs copies of his auto-biographies, Hudsons, New Street, 1978.

Newscaster, Angela Rippon, prepares to switch on the lights of the Coca Cola advert, around the summit of the Rotunda, 6th May 1981.

Bargain hunters at Lewis's, December 1980.

w Street, with Burlington Passage on the left and Needless
ley on the right, October 1982.

Corporation Street, going down towards the Central Fire Station, January 1984.

About 2,000 people queue to get into the Kempico store, at the start of its final closing sale, Bull Street, 6th January 1984. The store was originally known as Debenhams and prior to that Greys.

Crowds braved the cold to queue for hours outside the Virgin Megastore, the second largest record shop in Europe, when it opened today.

The store in Corporation Street, Birmingham, is the latest venture for the head of the Virgin group, Mr. Richard Branson, who arrived to perform the opening ceremony. 30·11·85

Film star, Joan Collins, arrives to sign copies of her book "Prime Time", W.H. Smith & Son Ltd., Union Street, 8th January 1985.

The Earl and Countess Spencer, Hudsons (now Dillons), New Street, 27th September 1986.

The Pavilions, High Street, November 1987.

...ebrating Birmingham's Centenary, in Victorian ...tume, are Barbara Wheeler, Juliet Burgese and ...en Burchell, with greetings from Senior Porter, ...lcolm Jones, Great Western Arcade, 11th January ...39.

Jasper Carrott poses with Mrs Ann Stokes and Michael, Hudsons, New Street, 5th November 1988.

125

TV Personality, Rustie Lee, signs autographs in The Pallasades, 5th December 1986. She was taking part in TV-am's Caring Christmas Campaign.

## Author Alton signs on

Author Alton Douglas will be signing copies of his latest book, 'Birmingham Remembered' at Hornby's in The Pallasades on Saturday, December 3rd.

'Birmingham Remembered', which commemorates the city's centenary, is published by The Birmingham Post & Mail Ltd.

Mr. Douglas's signing will be at 10.00 am. 1988

A "forgotten" section of Birmingham city centre once branded an eyesore has been turned into a prestigious shopping area.

Fletcher's Walk, Paradise Circus, is due to be officially opened tomorrow by Councillor Albert Bore, chairman of the city's economic development committee. 22.7.87

City Plaza, December 1989.

Andrew Betts regularly entertains shoppers at
the City Plaza, Cannon Street, 1991.

# CITY PLAZA

*Shopping in Style...*

LOWER GROUND FLOOR
BENETTON UOMO
HENRY'S
DILLONS
UPPER GROUND FLOOR
BETTY BARCLAY
JAEGER MAN
JAEGER LADIES
JONES BOOTMAKER
MONDI
C D MUSIC CENTRE
MONSOON
EVERYMOOD
CAPOLITO ROMA
THE ULTIMATE BARBER
STEFANEL
FOOD TERRACE
DUTCH DELIGHTS
LE BUFFET
PALMS PIANO BAR
2ND FLOOR ATRIUM COURT
TAO BEAUTY CLINIC

*BETWEEN CORPORATION ST. & ST PHILLIPS PLACE*
*Tel: 021 633 3969*

Film star, Sophia Loren, is presented with flowers at a signing session to promote her "Women & Beauty" book, Hudsons (now Dillons) New Street, 1984.

## ACKNOWLEDGEMENTS
(for providing photographs, for encouragement and numerous other favours)

Alfred Allen (Furnishers)Ltd; Ron Allso; Ansells Ltd., Property Dept.; Audrey and Graham Axford; The Bathroom Village; Anthony Bayliss; Bee Cee Enterprises; Andrew Betts; Birmingham City Council, Dept. of Planning and Architecture; Birmingham Post & Mail Ltd., Birmingham Reference Library, Local Studies; Nell Blackburn; Colin Bragg; Cadbury Schweppes Ltd.; Dave Carpenter; Central Midland Co-operative Society Ltd.; City Plaza (Birmingham) Ltd.; John and Jacqueline Coxell; Alan and Brenda Cronshaw; Michael Davies; Reg Davies; Dillons the Bookstore, New Street; Ed Doolan; Alison Emery; Tony Felmingham; John Frost Ltd.; Reg Gower; Val Hastings; HMSO, Birmingham; Karen Hicklin; Fred Holliday; Anne Jennings; Dave and Thelma Jones; Lassiters; Sue Letts; Lord Mayor's Parlour; Dennis Moore; Ordnance Survey; Mollie Payne; Natalie Powell; Eric Reeves; Barbara Silvester; Norman and Josie Smith; Brenda Treagust; H.G. Turner Ltd.; Stanley Webb; West Heath Pet Stores; Nancy Weston; Maurice White; Bob and Joan Wilkes; Rosemary Wilkes; Vera Woodfield.

Please forgive any possible omissions. Every effort has been made to include all organisations and individuals involved in the book.

Back cover:

New Street, c. 1935.

Golden Hillock Road, with Wordsworth Road on the right, Small Heath, 1920.